Capsule Craze:

The Comprehensive Guide to Building a Capsule Wardrobe

Rebecca Ellington

Table of Contents

CHAPTER 1:

Introduction

What Are Capsule Wardrobes?

Picture this: It's Friday night, and you're once again standing stoically in front of your closet door with your mouth agape, blankly staring at the pieces on your hangers. You threw on a sweater earlier, but it's much too warm for that. You opted for a dress, but you don't have any heels to match. On your bed is the pile of rejected outfits that you tried on minutes before. And accessories? Forget about it. You knew you should have gone to the mall and found a new trendy outfit, but who has the time or the money to do that every week?

You've already showered, applied your makeup, and fixed your hair as your date is waiting at the front door, growing impatient by the minute. Why, oh why, is it so hard to find something to wear?

What you should have done is built yourself a high functioning, easily adaptable, Capsule Wardrobe.

Oh, you haven't heard? Capsule Wardrobes are IN, and given that they've been around for over thirty years. They probably aren't going anywhere anytime soon.

If you're unfamiliar with the term, then you're in the right place.

Most women consider clothing old after wearing them up to

three times, and in some cases, like with wedding or party dresses, pieces are only worn once. With the advancements in technology, the push for fast fashion drives the industry as abroad clothing manufactures are used to cut costs. Designers who use to focus on the four-season styles have found themselves churning out styles more often now.

This cultural trend has manifests itself into compulsive buying and keeping costs affordable for the consumer. With the use of cheaper materials, the one-time-use phase has begun resulting to clutter and waste.

This culture has made women believe that they need to have a closet chock full of options, when in reality, having more choices at one's disposal leads to indecisiveness, stress, and ultimately, less satisfaction.

Capsule Wardrobes are trend-driven designers' greatest nightmare and everybody else's secret weapon when it comes to reusable, interchangeable, and high-quality staple pieces for any and every occasion. The purpose is to help women refine their cluttered wardrobes to include only high-quality essential pieces that can be worn and re-worn as much as they'd like.

The idea is to fill one's closet with timeless pieces that can be mixed and matched to create a plethora of outfits. If you've done your capsule correctly, you should need a total of thirty pieces in your wardrobe.

Think about how many outfits that are currently hanging in your closet right now. Do you think you can reduce them to thirty?

With this comprehensive guide, we're going to show you step-by-step how to do that.

CHAPTER 2:

History

Where Did Capsule Wardrobe Come From?

In the 1970s, fashion choices were bold, empowering, and verging on strange. Icons like Cher and Joni Mitchell sought creative recognition while gracing stages in flared out jeans, tie-dyed shirts, platform shoes and fringed, suede jackets. It was a time that begged for attention from anyone who was willing to give it, and it was almost as wild as it was freeing for designers of the day.

Meanwhile, in a small London boutique called Wardrobe, owner Susie Faux was igniting a new trend that stood out in stark contrast to the outlandish styles that were flooding the streets. While developing the next big wave in the fashion industry, she couldn't have predicted the implications that were about to emerge.

In all the hustle and bustle, Susie Faux saw the necessity for a different approach to fashion; one that was simpler, more subdued, and interchangeable with London's drastic seasonal changes. It is here that she developed and coined the term Capsule Wardrobe.

The idea behind Wardrobe was to create an all-in-one shop of essentials, where professional women could shop with confidence and find every item they might require in a single standalone location. Susie Faux, as it would turn out, would become the "godmother" of classic fashion innovation as her clients quickly become trusted friends and loyal customers. She sold staple pieces and inspired women around her.

As the daughter and granddaughter of two master tailors, her eye for high-quality fashion was ingrained from an early age. In adulthood, as a respected member of the London fashion community, she quickly became known for introducing British women to up and coming designers that would soon become international sensations such as Gianfranco Ferre and Jil Sander.

The concept was later popularized by American designer, Donna Karan, who is touted as being the woman who launched the concept of capsule wardrobes into the western world and, eventually, worldwide. In the mid-1980s, she released an influential collection of seven interchangeable work-wear pieces

Today, the term is continually referenced in newspapers, magazines, and fashion editorials proving it has achieved the coveted renowned status that many designers and fashion innovators can only hope for. As for Susie Faux, she is regularly complimented for being the woman who made it all possible.

Susie Faux

CHAPTER 3:

The Benefits of Capsule Wardrobes

There are many benefits to reducing the footprint of your wardrobe, and some of them are not as obvious as simply as clearing the clutter.

Have you ever noticed how self-made millionaires and innovators like Mark Zuckerberg are always caught wearing the same thing? Even mentioning his name, I bet you've envisioned the curly-haired technology guru in his casual hoodie sweater, a pair of jeans and lightweight sneakers. How about Apple founder Steve Jobs with his turtleneck sweaters? Even former President Barack Obama admitted that he limited his suit options to those of the black and blue variety. Admittedly, there must be something to this way of life.

What those successful people have realized that we're all slowly catching up on is that reducing the amount of time your brain spends mulling over insignificant details tend to waste time and energy that would be better utilized for the more complex decisions in our day-to-day.

Simply put, less is more. But why?

It Reduces Decision Fatigue

Decision fatigue is the inevitable deterioration of quality decision making made by individuals who have been participating in long sessions of decision making. It's something everyone experiences, even those with the best of intentions, and it's familiar that you are experiencing it every single day. That 2 p.m. afternoon crash at the office, anyone?

By reducing the overall amount of daily decision making, mental clarity is enhanced. The results are more productive days where you can be confident in the making decisions that are not being clouded by fatigue.

It Wastes Less Time

The average woman spends 16 minutes every weekday morning trying to decide what to wear, and about 14 minutes every weekend morning. If that doesn't sound considerable amount of time to you, then give these scenarios a thought: midday outfit changes as she runs from the office to dinner, or to the gym, date nights, parties, or unexpected accidents like spilling a beverage on a blouse that prompts an immediate outfit swap.

All in all, women spend 287 days out of their life thinking about what to drape over their body; think about what they could do with all that extra time if they reduced their overall decision making by creating a more limited wardrobe.

It Reduces Stress

Fumbling about in your bedroom as you struggle to determine if your outfit is too formal, too casual, too short, or too long for whatever event you're about to head out for, increases stress, anxiety, and reduces self-esteem as your decision making is being challenged. Given that stress has been shown to increase the risk of obesity, depression and heart disease, limiting our sources of stress is highly beneficial to our overall health.

It Wastes Less Energy

Not only do large, complicated wardrobes beckon for more decision making, but they also require more upkeep and maintenance to stay organized. Think about all the time you spend just shuffling your summer clothing to the back of the rack to make your fall and winter styles more accessible and apparent as the seasons change. Also, having fewer pieces overall means less time spent sorting through your laundry bins as you prepare them for a wash and less time afterward as you fold and press them for storage.

It Inspires Confidence

When you force yourself to create a more focused wardrobe, you're forcing yourself to take a good, long look at your style and the kind of pieces that not only make you look good but feel good, too.

Think of your closet as a luxurious five-star restaurant; the menu might only be a single page, but rest assured, every single ingredient and spice was chosen with a purpose -- to create the best-tasting dishes. Compare that to when you visit a large-family chain like iHop where, while the possibilities are seemingly endless, they are bland, generic and uninspired. When you're a victim of fast fashion, that's what your wardrobe starts to look like. Leaving you feeling like nothing fits right or looks good enough to bother wearing.

When you're sure of your style, you're sure of yourself, and that confidence will manifest itself throughout additional parts of your life such as relationships with your family and your job.

It Saves Money

We touched earlier on how new fashionable trends created a culture of fast fashion, making buying new pieces affordable for the average consumer. But, when those pieces are worn once or twice, how much are you really saving? The answer is, not much at all. By creating a small collection of essentials, you'll save upwards of 75% of your current shopping budget, leaving you with significantly more financial freedom.

As you can see, building a capsule wardrobe has the potential to improve your life. Not only by reducing your overall stress, but by building your confidence and making your day-to-day more manageable. You'll save time and considerable amounts of money by making it easier to fine-tune your style, and before long, strangers in the street will be wondering how you became such a fashion-forward success.

CHAPTER 4:

Questions to Ask Yourself Before Building Your Capsule Wardrobe

While building a capsule wardrobe is an exciting event, you may still be wondering if it's something that would benefit you. To help you determine if you should take the capsule plunge, there are a few questions you should ask yourself. After all, it's that impulsive nature that led to your out-of-control shopping habits and clothes collection anyway.

1. **Do you sometimes have difficulty finding something to wear?**

   You know what we're talking about, standing in front of your stacked-to-the-brim closet as the dread creeps upon you, realizing you have absolutely nothing to wear! Having too many options can completely overwhelm our senses leading to stress, anxiety, and a strong urge to run to the mall for binge shopping. If you find yourself in this predicament, it's time to declutter that closet and make room for a capsule.

2. **Would having more time in the morning benefit you?**

   For many people, every minute counts. Would having an extra ten or twenty minutes in the morning make starting your day a little easier? Taking the difficult decision making out of the equation can add up big time, and a capsule wardrobe could be the quick fix you need.

9

3. **Do you want to save some money?**

If your credit card is getting out of control while you try to keep up with the latest trends, consider downsizing to high-quality, practical pieces that can be interchanged throughout the year. This could help you get a handle on your finances or even make it possible for that dream vacation you keep telling yourself you'll one day take.

4. **Are you tired of putting on old clothes that don't compliment your personality, body type, and style?**

When you have a closet full of clothes, it's easy to overlook some of your pieces Before long, you might not even fit into half of them, or they've been washed and rewashed many times that the material has worn down making them completely unwearable. That's one of the downfalls of fast fashion and why capsule wardrobes focus on well-made clothing that is built to last. By choosing essentials that'll complement your shape, you're far less likely to put on a top only to remove it because you don't like the way it makes you feel. If you want to regain confidence in yourself and your style, capsule wardrobes can help.

5. **Do you worry about the footprint your fast fashion choices are creating?**

In order for manufacturers to churn out many new styles regularly throughout the year, compromises are often made with regards to the quality of the clothes, to how factory workers are compensated and treated. Taking control of your fashion purchases can make an impact globally, and minimizing your wardrobe can help you focus on brands and designers you believe in.

If you answered yes to any of the above questions, it's time to start talking about how to structure your first capsule wardrobe.

CHAPTER 5:

The Structure of Your Capsule

Building a framework to work from is the ultimate key to a successful capsule wardrobe. It should consist of a small selection of carefully selected pieces to help you express your style while being functional for your lifestyle to quickly grab your clothes and go on any given day.

To help you determine the structure of your capsule, we've outlined the four key areas of considerations for your framework.

Concept

First, you're going to want to look ahead to the coming season and ask yourself what you want your style to look like. This is a fun exercise that forces you to forget about what you already wear, because you own it, and think about what you want to wear because of its functionality within your day-to-day, and the confidence you want to exude out into the world. For example, if it's turning to fall and you know you love to wear high boots, leggings and long sweaters, include these here. (We'll cover these accessories in Chapter 14.)

It is here that you're going to want to create a long list of the elements you hope to include in your capsule -- colors, textures, and fabrics. Narrowing down the specifics of your likes and dislikes will save you time in the long run. Moreover, brainstorming will help you get excited about what your finished capsule will look like, which will serve as a great motivation throughout the process.

It might be beneficial to create a mood board to play around with different themes and ideas until you feel confident in your decision.

Uniform

Once you have determined an overall concept, it's time to create one functional uniform, or outfit formula, that you can see yourself wearing. Remember that Barack Obama narrowed down his daily style to blue and black three-piece suits.

You may already have a uniform without consciously being aware of it. If you're having trouble coming up with one, ask yourself these questions:

1. Do you tend to reach for the same pair of jeans to go out and run errands because they're loose and comfortable?
2. Do you have an addiction to vintage dresses?
3. Do you put on the same sweater whenever you're feeling a little chilly?

If you can pinpoint specific items to particular situations, you're well on your way to determining your uniform. Determining your uniform is a fundamental starting point for any capsule wardrobe project and you'll want to include several items in it. Don't just focus on pants and tops, but include shoes, bags, and jewelry, too.

Build the Framework

Now that you understand your outfit style, it's time to put together the other basic essentials your wardrobe will require to be functional. We'll use your uniform and the elements you set out in your concept to get us started.

Ex. 1. Framework

Uniform:
T-Shirt, Jeans, Sneakers

Concept Elements:
Boots, Leggings, Long Sleeve Shirts

When building the framework, you should estimate how many of each item you will require, aiming between twenty and thirty pieces in total. These can always be adjusted so don't worry about overestimating, just give your best-educated guess.

Key Things to Keep in Mind

You will want to have several versions of each item in your uniform. A good starting point is to allocate 50% of your overall items to the categories your uniform fall under.

Consider how often you will be reaching for the other items in your capsule and distribute accordingly. If it seems unlikely you will need to wear a dress more than once in the upcoming season, you don't need five different dresses.

Items that require more frequent washing should be considered of higher importance than those that require infrequent washing. If your hoodie can survive five days without a wash, you will need less of them overall, as opposed to things like underwear that require frequent washing.

Regularly worn items like shoes and jackets will have a longer life and need to be replaced less often if they are rotated every couple of days; allocating at least three items to these categories will benefit you in the long run.

Ex. 2. Structure

T-Shirt	Longsleeves	Jeans	Leggings	Sneakers	Boots	Jacket	Dresses
5	5	4	2	2	2	3	2

As you can see above, the uniform (t-shirts, jeans, and sneakers) categories had the highest quantities, while the upcoming seasonal came second. I added in a couple extras I see myself wanting to wear a couple of times like the dresses, for good measure.

Draft Your Final Capsule

Using your basic structure guide above and the concept you visualized for yourself, get more specific about your capsule and start narrowing down colors and textures.

Ex. 3. Drafting

T-Shirts	5	(2) White (2) Black Scoopneck (1) Red V-Neck
Longsleeves	5	(2) Black (2) Grey Crewneck (1) Red Stripes
Jeans	4	(1) Black Skinny (1) Blue Loose Fit (1) Blue Slim Fit (1) Ripped
Leggings	2	(1) Black (1) Grey
Sneakers	2	(1) Black Runners (1) White Casual
Boots	2	(1) Black, Knee-High (1) Suede Ankle
Jackets	3	(1) Blue Denim (1) Windbreaker (1) Black, Leather
Dresses	2	(1) Short Sleeves, Cotton, Floor Length (1) Longsleeves, lace, scooped

Drafting Tips:

1. Look at what you already own, pull them out, and separate the items that already fall within your capsule specifications. If your style was already well defined, you might be able to build most of your capsule with items you already own.
2. Examine the categories you've outlined in sets to help determine a good balance of neutrals/bright colors and basics/statement pieces for optimization.
3. Keep a list of your final draft on hand for future reference, keeping a careful note of items that need to be repaired, replaced, or bought in the future. This can ensure your capsule remains tidy and organized so you don't find yourself buying unnecessary pieces.

Color Palette

Base Tones

It's important to spend ample time figuring out what color you feel most comfortable in as this will help you determine your base tone. Think about what colors you tend to reach for when you're shopping, and think about which colors can easily adapt to the changing seasons.

The main tones most women base their capsule wardrobes on are neutrals like:

- Black
- Beige
- White
- Navy
- Tan

Highlights & Accents

It is inevitable that you will have days where neutrals won't do the trick, and it's on these days you'll want to ensure you have ample accents and highlights to accentuate your pieces.

These accent tones will serve to complement your base and help you transition into the changing seasons. Feel free to use the color palette guide below in order to best determine the most complimentary accent colors for your wardrobe.

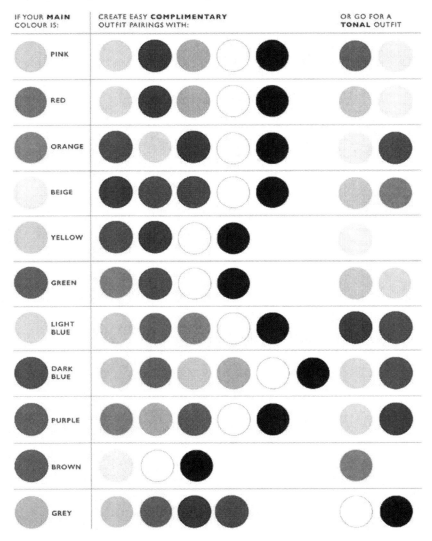

CHAPTER 6:

Shopping the Right Way

Shopping can be an overwhelming experience, even the most regular of consumers, and even more so for those that are embarking on building their first capsule wardrobe. But it doesn't have to be. If you've fallen victim to the appeal of the fast fashion world, you're going to require a bit of rewiring. To assist with that we've compiled six helpful tips to shop the right way for the ultimate capsule building experience.

1. **Be Frugal**

   An easy way to reduce your expenses while still finding high-quality pieces for your capsule is to shop at local consignment stores or thrift shops. This is particularly useful if one of the reasons you've decided to become a capsule queen is to reduce your fashion footprint. Shopping second-hand makes use of items that would otherwise go to waste and end up in a landfill, and they're usually heavily marked down to encourage shoppers to purchase them. This means you can save a few bucks all the while feeling confident that you're shopping mindfully and making the best use of already available resources.

   Before you plan a trip to your local mall, poke your head into some second-hand stores -- they can be a treasure trove. You can never be sure what you will find, making it an exhilarating experience, and a frugal one. You might find that you have a special love for rescuing second-hand goods, too.

2. Go Vintage

Online shopping is another fantastic avenue for sustainable fashion choices that won't break the bank. With the increased popularity of online boutiques like Etsy, you can find completely new styles or old vintage buys with the click of the button. It's easier than ever to locate and purchase high-quality pieces that can really make your capsule pop.

Since they're vintage, it's less likely you'll run into somebody with the same piece as you, further assisting in developing a personal style that you can be proud of.

3. Quality, Not Quantity

Not all your new buys have to come from second-hand stores. In fact, you might be someone who wants to avoid them altogether, which is completely fine, too. As long as you are being mindful of the quality of the pieces you are selecting, you can still shop at whatever modern, trendy store you like. Although, be wary of "too good to be true" sales like two-for-ones. They seem like great deals because they save you money, but if the quality of the piece isn't there it's likely to wear out after a wash or two.

In addition, if you're reducing your wardrobe for ethical reasons, you'll want to do further research into the brands you love to ensure that they're meeting the same ethical considerations you have for yourself. If your high-quality jacket is made in a rundown sweatshop, do you still want to buy it? That's only one example of the questions you'll want to ask yourself as you search for your new look.

4. Bring a List

Just like you do when you go to the grocery store, bringing a list of the items you need to purchase will help keep you focused on the task at hand and away from the flashy deal signs designed to encourage you to buy. If you've drafted your capsule correctly, you should have a clear idea of what you're looking for when ypu go shopping. Take the extra few minutes to fine-tune your list before you start opening your wallet.

5. Be Sale Savvy

Be aware of your favorite brands marketing techniques. In the digital age, many stores will offer you 10% or 15% off your first sale by adding your e-mail to their promotional mailing list, or digitally check-in to their store's social media page. Do that at every store you shop at, and those numbers can add up!

They might even have the recommend-a-friend deals, too, benefiting both you and your capsule building bestie. By staying aware of new deals and sale opportunities, you can ensure you're getting the most bang for your buck even when you're shopping at pricier stores.

6. Focus on Fit, Not Size

Building your capsule is supposed to encourage you to look beyond the size tags and focus on the more important things:

- Does that top fit you well and enhance your natural beauty?
- Are you comfortable wearing those jeans?

The fashion industry has conditioned us to believe that larger sizes lower our self-worth, but considering how much your size can differentiate from store to store, isn't it time you stopped focusing on the number and started focusing on the fit?

Since the main purpose of a capsule wardrobe is to end up with fewer pieces than you began with, it's vital that the choices you make are items you see yourself in regularly., If you are humming and hawing about whether or not a dress or a top look good on you, don't commit to it until you're positive it does.

Starter Pieces

Now that we understand how to shop the right way, let's talk a bit about starter pieces, or the basics of your capsule.

Your starter pieces are your go-to essentials you can see yourself wearing again and again without feeling like you've overused them. This might be your favorite tee or a pullover that you cannot live without.

The basics of your capsule are going to come down to three key factors: **style, fit, and fabric.**

Since your basics are what you tend to wear the most, it's important to choose pieces that use high-quality fabrics that will last. Otherwise, you'll find yourself replacing them more frequently than you might want to; something you want to avoid if saving money is important to you.

When you're seeking your basics, remember that these should complement your bold looks. Focus on neutral tones you can easily pair with your other items.

When selecting your basics, consider the minor weight fluctuations your body goes through on a regular basis and plan accordingly. These pieces should have enough wiggle room that you feel comfortable in them when your weight raises slightly or on a day where you might feel a little bloated, but they should also fit comfortably on days when your weight is stable.

When picking your starter pieces, ask yourself:

1. Do I love this so much I'll wear it until it falls apart?
2. Does it pair well with my other pieces?
3. Can I live without it?
4. Is it made to last?

With your basics determined, you're well on your way to building your versatile capsule wardrobe.

CHAPTER 7:

Closet Care & Maintenance to Get the Most Out of What You Have

Since you'll be downsizing your wardrobe as you build your capsule, you're probably thinking it will be a breeze to maintain your closet and your pieces. While that may be true on a quantity level, there are still a few things you should keep in mind to ensure you're getting the longest possible life out of your small collection.

Wear Undershirts

Wearing undershirts will assist with keeping your shirts clean and free of things like pesky sweat stains. Additionally, they'll make your see-through items (i.e. white shirts) opaque so you can wear them with confidence.

Wash Frugally

We can get away with wearing our clothing a couple of times before they're due for a trip to the laundry, unless we were working out hard in them or they've fallen victim to a spill.

Over washing your clothes can make them fade or lose their shape sooner. By washing them when it is necessary, you can extend their wearing life.

Choose the Right Products

You can help keep your clothes intact by being mindful of the types of products you're using the clean them with. Gentle, non-toxic products made with natural ingredients can preserve the look of your clothing. For utmost care, be sure to carefully read the washing specifications labeled on your items before throwing them in a load to avoid shrinking or damage.

Hand Wash/Line Dry

In addition to choosing the right products, omit the high-powered washer entirely. Gentle hand washing your clothes will help increase the odds that your items will keep that store-bought feel and look. The kinder we are to our clothes, the longer they'll want to stick around with us.

Keep a Working Wardrobe List

We briefly touched on the idea of keeping a working wardrobe list earlier, but it's such a great way to keep your closet under control and organized. Your working wardrobe list should be regularly referenced to see which items in your capsule are beginning to show wear and tear, and should be replaced or repaired. Having this neatly laid out makes the upkeep of your closet easy since you know what items require urgent attention. Practicing this can help reassure you don't find yourself bolting to the mall for a replacement that may not fit your capsule theme.

CHAPTER 8:

Pairing Your Body Type with Your Outfit

Even the most confident women tend to have areas on their bodies they're not 100% in love with. And while it's important not to get negative or obsessive about these areas, there are things you can do that will make you feel proud of your personal style.

Accentuating your most liked features by choosing outfits that enhance than minimize those areas. This gives you a confidence and self-esteem boost, so it's worthwhile to give your fit significant consideration.

The first step to create a look that accents the right areas of your body is to figure out what kind of body yours closely resembles. Stand in front of a full-length mirror, or ask a friend, to help you walk through the five main body types to determine which one is yours. Remember, there is no wrong answer because they're all beautiful.

The Five Main Body Types:

Pear

Pear-shaped people tend to have hips that are wider than their shoulders and a small waist. If you find that when buying items, like skirts for instance, they fit your hips well but are too large around your waist, you are likely pear-shaped.

Straight

Sometimes referred to as a column-body, straight shaped people have shoulders that perfectly aligns with their hips. There tends to be little to no waist definition, and a flat bottom.

Apple

Apple shapes, like straight shapes, have little to no waist definition, but they tend to have more rounded and wider shoulders. If you think your shoulders are broad for your frame, you are likely an apple.

Hourglass

Hourglass shaped people are also referred to as curvy, given their obvious waist definition, wide shoulders and wide hips. Measuring your waist and your hips to determine if you fall into this category as it is not always obvious.

Strawberry

Strawberry shaped people, or inverted triangle, generally have wide shoulders that exceed the width of their hips, flat bottoms, and small waists. An easy way to find out if you fit this body type is if you generally buy larger sized clothing for your tops than you do your bottoms.

Dressing for Your Body

There are no real rules to what you can or can't wear. However, some styles suit different shapes better than others. If you're looking to better define your clothing to fit your body, these general rules below will help lead you on the journey.

Pear

Since your hips get attention, it's time to focus on the top half of your body.

When selecting things for your top half, whether it's a jacket or a blouse, try to make sure the hemline doesn't fall at the widest part of your frame, as this will further accentuate the pear frame.

Choose bootcut, or straight-legged pants and A-line dresses and skirts.

If you like to wear stripes, focus on horizontal stripes for your top half and avoid them for your bottoms. Horizontal stripes tend to elongate the part of the body they're worn on.

When layering, use heavier textures and fabrics on your top half but not your bottoms.

Pear Clothing Tips

- Wear wide-hemmed pants, skirts, and dresses.
- Light on top, dark on Bottom for greater contrast.
- Necklines best suited to your shape are a cowl, boat, and square.
- Strapless dresses.
- Ruffles on top will look great on you.
- Don't wear jackets that fall below your waist where possible.
- Pointy-shoes will give your legs length.

Straight

Your slim hips make jeans look fabulous, so feel free to experiment with a variety of denim.

Straight lines will further accentuate your figure, so A-Line or narrow pleated skirts and dresses typically work best.

Avoid items that try hard to add curves. Avoid textures (i.e. frills), or anything bulky and wide.

Fitted shirts and clean cotton fabrics on top will sit nicely on your frame.

Straight Clothing Tips

- Long jackets will embellish your straight stature.
- Find tops with ruffles and collars to accentuate your chest.
- Add dimensions by utilizing layers.
- Scoop necklines and sweetheart tops help create the illusion of curves.
- Clothing with side crunch or rucking looks great on you.
- Brightly colored bottoms will further add dimension to your shape.

Apple

Simple and straight lines will be an added benefit if you have an apple body type. But you'll want your tops to be looser than those with straight body types.

Tunic style tops with well-fitted pants tend to work well to accentuate your legs while minimizing your shoulders.

A-Line dresses and pencil skirts tend to be well received.

Avoid sharp angles on your tops as they draw unwanted attention to your stomach and tend to make shoulders look wider.

Cardigans and swing-style coats without belts are ideal.

Apple Clothing Tips

- Monochromatic tones will look great.
- Elongate your torso with v-necklines
- Accessorize with belts to accentuate your waistline
- Seek out empire dress lines and tops
- Strengthen your shape with bootcut or flared jeans
- Short skirts will accentuate your legs

Hourglass

Hourglass-shaped people want to accentuate their curves.

Avoid loose clothing or anything heavy as they have a tendency to make hourglasses look larger than they are.

When selecting dresses and skirts, aim for ones with distinct waist definition, or accessorize with a belt.

For pants, you're in luck, as you can get away with most bottoms, but the more defined their shape is, the better.

- Focus on precisely tailored clothing to accentuate your

curves.

- Experiment with wrap-style dresses.
- Accessorize with belts to enhance your shape.
- Wear high-waisted skirts.
- Choose thin, light, fabrics.
- Straight legged pants or skinny jeans look great.

Strawberry

Strawberry-shapes should always tailor their outfits to accentuate their bottom halves. Well fitted jeans and pants are a must.

Straighter lined clothing that doesn't accentuate your shoulders is ideal.

Stiff fabrics work well with strawberry types, and sleeveless tops are recommended.

Stay away from anything with a wide neckline, or with stripes as they'll enhance the look of your broad shoulders.

Strawberry Clothing Tips

- Bright bottoms to accentuate your legs.
- Wide-hemmed on pants and skirts
- Full skirts look better than short skirts.
- Avoid thin straps like spaghetti-straps and boat necklines
- Wear high-waisted pants and skirts to aid in creating a more defined waistline

CHAPTER 9:

Capsule-On-The-Go: The Quick Guide for Getaways and Trips

You don't have to limit the use of capsule wardrobes to your day-to-day wear. They can be great when incorporated into compact carry-ons for your next vacation. Most people tend to over-pack their luggage because they're worried they'll forget something important and have an "Oh no!" moment on their trip. The truth is that rarely happens, and the excess outfits stay folded in the bottom of your suitcase for the duration of the trip. Let's save yourself the time, energy, and luggage space by building a condensed capsule for your next getaway.

Travel Capsule Packing Tips

1. Only pack what you truly love

Just as with your everyday capsule, you want to clearly define what you're naturally driven to wear in the climate you'll be traveling to. If you love the color of the bikini you bought last summer but feel uncomfortable wearing it, don't include it in your travel capsule. Focus on what fits you well and makes you feel good as pieces that don't will be left unworn.

2. Pick a color scheme

Choose a color scheme before you start packing. This way all your items match by creating a wide variety of outfit options.

3. Limit your shoes and handbags

Most capsule wardrobes limit the number of shoes you can have, and your travel capsule is no exception. In fact, it should be even stricter!

On most vacations, you won't require more than two pairs of shoes. That's one pair of sneakers, or casual walking shoes, and one pair specific to your destination. If you're heading to the beach, this might be a pair of flip-flops or sandals. But if you're heading to the mountains, a pair of sturdy boots would be more appropriate. Use your best judgment here.

And handbags? You'll need your purse or backpack to carry your wallet, phone, and passport in. You probably don't need those two totes, a beach bag, and a backpack, too. Try to limit yourself to only one handbag or backpack; you'll be amazed as to how efficient it is.

4. Consider chameleon pieces

Wardrobe chameleons are those items that can be dressed up or dressed down, being interchangeable for different situations that might arise. While we're not advocating for you to bring a chameleon piece for every "what-if" scenario, we are encouraging the consideration of pieces like long sleeve t-shirts that can be rolled up in milder temperatures or put under sweaters for cooler nights.

With all that in mind, it's time to build your travel capsule.

Step 1: Basic Structure

Start with your basic structure as we did with your everyday capsule. These essential items are going to include the clothing you decide to wear in transit, so bear in mind what method of transportation you will be using.

Your basic travel capsule should consist of:

✓ **Three** tops

Pack a formal, elbow-length or long sleeve, and [insert other shirt here] for a variety of occasions.; one ¾" length sleeve or long sleeve, depending on the destination climate. Even when you're traveling down south where the evenings are considerably warmer than you're used to, it's good to have a long sleeve shirt to protect you from pesky mosquitos.

✓ **Two** bottoms

Pack a pair of formal, casual, and full-length pants. If you have an unexpectedly cool, rainy weather, you'll be thankful you packed at least one pair of long pants.

✓ **One** sweater or jacket
✓ **One** scarf
✓ **One** pair of sneakers or walking shoes

If you're expecting inclement weather, some form of rain protection should be included, too.

Step 2: Additional Items

Once you've established your core capsule, you can start incorporating some extra items you think will be useful for your trip. An example of extras includes a dress, formal footwear, an additional top or sweater, or an extra skirt or pair of shorts.

Step 3: Accessorize

Finally, it's time to jazz up those outfits with stylish accessories. Since accessories are known to dramatically change the look of an outfit, it's important to include them as part of your capsule. This ensures you have the most options out of the least amount of clothing items.

A couple of accessories to consider including in your capsule are belts, necklaces, bracelets, earrings, and leggings.

Step 4: Review

Now that you've collected all your pieces for your travel capsule, you'll want to review everything you have chosen and make sure that it makes sense with your travel destination and the kind of activities you plan on participating in.

Ask yourself these questions:

1. What do I want to wear on the plane/bus/boat/car?
2. What will I wear if attending a formal dinner and party?
3. What do I need for my rock climbing/snorkeling/hiking excursion?
4. What will I wear to historical sights, museums, and shops?
5. Do I have something in case I get cold/hot/rains?

If you've done your due diligence, you're able to pack lighter than you used to (a bonus if you've been subjected to pay hefty fees for overweight luggage!) and you'll use everything that you bring.

Another point to consider is, depending on the duration of your trip, if you'll be able to do some laundry while you're away. If you're able to do laundry, limit your travel capsule items as you can reuse those items after washing

CHAPTER 10:

Transition Pieces
You'll Want to Have

While some people prefer to divide up their capsule into things like "A Work-Ready" Capsule and an "Everyday Casual" Capsule, or a "Spring Capsule" and a "Summer Capsule", it can quickly get out of hand and disorganized. This can diminish the functionality of your capsule and encourage you to buy new pieces.

With a truly successful capsule, you should have a wide variety of pieces that can be utilized in many settings and seasons.

As you work through the year, make a note of what pieces can be used in the next season. This extra bit of attention will be instrumental in keeping your wardrobe small while maximizing its potential for usability.

From the Office to the Party

If your office or workplace has a dress code, it's best to start ensuring you have all the necessary essentials to meet those guidelines set out by your employer.

Once you've established them, you can focus on what transition pieces can be integrated effectively.

Transition Tips: Layer, Swap & Accessorize

One of the easiest ways to transform your work attire into a more relaxed look for evening is to utilize accessories. As we mentioned before, accessories have the ability to make any outfit look completely different by adding or taking away pieces. Bring a complimentary necklace and a pair of matching earrings to kick your appearance up a notch after you've left the office.

Swapping out those heels for a neutral flat-footed shoe makes it possible for you to dance the night away.

Layering is another technique for a quick and easy fix. By adding a colorful cardigan or a denim jacket over your work blouse can dressdown your look while still appearing put together.

CHAPTER 11:

Changing Seasons Seamlessly (From Spring to Summer, from Fall to Winter and Back Again: Making the Most of Your Capsule Year-Round)

Let's start by assuming you built your first capsule wardrobe in the spring.

Below, we'll go through the four seasons and suggest ways to seamlessly morph your capsule into a functional summer wardrobe, then into fall as the weather drops, and finally into the long, cold days of winter.

Of course, this is only to serve as a guideline, as our personal capsule might have a need or function, depending on your lifestyle.

Spring Essentials You'll Use in Summer

First, let's look at what you have included in your spring capsule. If you haven't, consider developing your capsule when the time is right.

1. Basic t-shirt

Everybody needs a high-quality t-shirt as part of their spring capsule. Those warmer days tend to sneak up on us and you'll want something that is functional, with or without a sweater. Choose a style (V-neck, scoop or crew) and stick to it. If you followed the body type guide appropriately, you should know which neckline is flattering on you. Stick with solid colors or neutrals for optimal versatility.

2. Rain Boots

Spring means showers (and as the song goes, then come the flowers). If your region is known to get a sprinkle, invest in a good pair of rain boots anyway. It is an essential item to every spring capsule and you'll be ready for action when the rain starts.

3. White Jeans

Spring is the season of new beginnings and what better way to start those beginnings than with a crisp pair of white jeans? White is fabulous because it pairs well with every color -- neutrals to pastels and neon, and everything in between. Since we're in spring, look for a thick pair that isn't opaque, but not too thick to cause your legs to sweat.

4. Denim Jacket

Aside from being a great way to keep the wind away in the spring, denim jackets are very versatile pieces you can include in your wardrobe, making it an extra essential to your capsule. Denim can be used to make a dress look casual, or it can serve to add some edge. It happens to work best without the one spring essential: the basic t-shirt. IIf you don't already have one, I recommend it.

5. Trench Coat

Trench coats are one of the most useful pieces you can include in your capsule because they can be utilized from spring through fall, depending on the weather. Include a neutral colored trench in your spring capsule you can see yourself wearing in other seasons, especially if that bright red trench from Saks is calling your name.

6. Sneakers, Wedges, and Flats

As you emerge from your winter hibernation, you're likely to find yourself spending more time outside, going on casual walks with friends as you bask in that welcoming spring sunshine. For that reason, your spring capsule should include a pair of good walking shoes or sneakers, a pair of wedges for dressier outings, and flats for when those tired feet just need to breathe.

7. Handbags

With those frequent trips to the local coffee shop or park, you'll need a functional handbag to help carry your important year-round items, like your wallet and keys. Again, try to stick with a neutral color here for adaptability to your spring collection into summer.

8. Sunglasses

We mentioned that spring sunshine, and we're going to reiterate - it's coming. Be prepared and protect your eyes with a pair of sunglasses you love and not in trend. Choose a frame that looks flawless on you, after all, our faces stay the same.

Summer Essentials You'll Use in Fall

As we drift from summer to fall, shorts, cropped pants, and skirts invites the chills as heavy sweaters brings on the sweats. These pieces are not right for the fall season as the weather can turn in an instance. When designing your summer capsule, bring in lighter sweaters and long pants to help fight off the chill when the season begins to change.

1. Basic t-shirt

Like we said above, you'll be thankful for your basic t-shirt in spring because you'll quickly understand their value; given how functional they can be. If you need replacing by the summer, do so, as you'll be able to wear it with many of your fall pieces, too.

2. Tank Top

The weather is cooling off and that doesn't mean it's time to put away all those tank tops. Keep these on hand through the fall to put under other shirts on chillier days or to layer underneath a jacket or cardigan for a fast and easy look.

3. Knee-Length Dress

A tank-style dress, for example, can be used frequently in the fall as it is in the summer, if you're one that prefers a cute dress in the warmer months. By ensuring you have at least one knee-length dress, you're preparing yourself to be comfortable both in the blistering heat and the cool, windy days.

4. Lightweight Jacket

A suede jacket or a blazer can make a casual look pop. They are super useful during the transition into fall as it becomes too cold to go without one. They can also be worn to make your work attire casual for a spontaneous night out.

Layering Tip:

As the weather starts to turn, start implementing layering techniques. Layering is the key to making your outfits transition in-between seasons. Ideally, you want these to pair well with all your styles and colors.

Fall Essentials You'll Use in the Winter

Moving from fall to winter is one of the least complicated changes your capsule will endure, especially if you are already equipped.

1. Long Sleeve T-shirts

It's good to have a long-sleeve t-shirt on hand because you're not always going to layer everything you're wearing. They're a great go-to to throw on when you're heading out to run some errands or hosting company at home. You'll also find yourself reaching for it when the winter chill sets in.

2. Sweater

For those days when a long-sleeve t-shirt isn't cutting it, a nice sweater can make your look formal when paired with a fine pair of slacks, or combine it with some loose-fitting jeans for a laid-back look.

3. Jeans

They don't have to be white, but you can already see how useful it is to have a well-fitting pair of jeans on hand. You'll use them in every season.

4. The LBD (Little Black Dress)

The closer we get to Thanksgiving and Christmas, you'll be invited to social events and dinner parties. A clean, fitted black dress will be worth investing in if you don't already own one.

Winter Essentials You'll Use in the Spring

We're coming full circle now. You'll notice that your spring capsule included the largest number of pieces, and that's not an accident since most of those pieces are being recycled into the seasons as you approach them.

1. Long Sleeve T-shirt

You'll certainly be grateful for your long sleeve t-shirts as you're cozying up to the fireplace, sipping your hot cocoa, and watching your favorite winter classics.

2. Cardigans

A cardigan sweater is a fantastic layering tool (and you probably already have one from your fall capsule collection). Go for quality here, as cardigans can easily be implemented into any look. You'll have difficulty keeping your hands away from it through the winter.

3. Jeans

If I had to create a capsule, I would include pieces that could be used year-round, and jeans are at the top of my list. Since it's used so frequently, sticking with a solid color like black or blue is ideal, if you don't want to invest in multiple pairs.

4. Boots

If you live in a snowy region, winter boots are a MUST. And as that snow starts to melt in the springtime, you'll still be using them, making them an important essential for your winter-spring transition.

There are no hard rules when it comes to choosing the pieces you can utilize year-round. It's important to take some time to consider what those pieces might be before you fine-tune your capsule. The extra legwork will help keep your closet organized while making transitioning between seasons a breeze.

CHAPTER 12:

Kid-friendly Capsules

Capsule wardrobes aren't just for adults; you can really get a handle on your children's cluttered closet space by adapting them to the capsule lifestyle while they're young. It's very easy to implement with kids as they require significantly fewer items day-to-day than we do. It's well worth the time to do to live minimally.

Kid's capsules, ideally, should have between twelve and fourteen items total. Their entire wardrobe can fit in a single dresser drawer. How's that for keeping tidy. Seasonally, that breaks down to having about six tops, five bottoms, and perhaps a dress if you have a little girl.

What Are the Benefits to Kid Capsules?

Much like our own capsules, there are many benefits to adopting the capsule lifestyle with your kids. With how quickly our kids grow out of their clothing, building a capsule is one of the most cost-effective decisions you can make. By carefully selecting your kids clothing pieces to be versatile and long-lasting, you'll save money over time, which can be used for other things like your kid's college fund.

You'll also be getting the most out of your purchases because instead of your kids constantly reaching for the same shirt or pair of pants, they'll be rotating their items on a regular basis.

If you've ever thought that you could use a few more minutes in the morning to get yourself and your kids ready for the day, shave off some pesky decision-making time and build them a capsule that'll ensure they look and feel their best every single morning.

The Six Key Questions to Ask Yourself When Building Your Child's Capsule

1. Is it simple?
2. Is it comfortable?
3. Is it built to last?
4. Is it flexible and versatile?
5. Is it affordable?

Building Your Child's Capsule

Pick a day where your kid is out of the house whether that's school, daycare, or on a playdate, and go through the closet. If you try to elimanate items from their exisiting wardrobe while they are there, they'll want to keep everything even if it doesn't fit anymore.

First, take all of your child's clothes and make sure they've been thoroughly washed. After folding, lay them out in front of you so you can see what you have and start connecting what your child will like to see in their capsule. If you're noticing a lot of blues, it's safe to say you should build your capsule around that hue; if you change your child's style drastically, there's a chance they won't like it and tantrums will ensue.

Make a collection of all the key items your child cannot do without as they tend to hold onto many sentimental items like sweaters from grandma's. If you have a plethora of these items, then you decide which items are more important than others. Until you're sure those items won't be missed, place those lesser-worn items in a box for safekeeping.

Making the Most Out of Your Pieces

As you know now, the more versatile the capsule is the better it serves you. Below are some helpful tips when choosing your colors and essentials.

1. **Base Color**

As mentioned earlier, if your child already has a love affair with a specific color, you'll likely want to tie that into your child's capsule and use it as a base. If your child is too young to know any different, then pull color palettes until you find one you like and inspiring. As with your own capsule, it's important to consider what colors work throughout the seasons to make shopping for replacements easier.

With that in mind, choose a base color for your child's capsule.

Black, gray, navy or brown tend to be good base colors for both boys and girls, although you'll likely notice that the girl's shades are lighter than the boys.

2. **Accent Colors**

Once you've decided on a neutral, choose two colors to accent the tone. If you chose a navy base, light gray's and blacks pair well. Or, for your girly-girls who can't let go of pink, pair them with blues and navy's.

3. **Patterns**

Choose three patterns you'd like to incorporate into their capsule theme. If you don't have an affinity to any patterns then stripes, florals, and polka dots are commonly recommended staples.

Kid-friendly Essentials

Now that you've determined your theme and colors, you're probably wondering how to break up your capsule and what essentials to have on hand. This will vary depending on where you live, so bear in mind any regional needs.

Tops

Have twice as many tops as you do bottoms. This will enable you to layer pieces, which are highly practical in the transitioning seasons, and it makes your child's style have added flare.

Shoes

If your child is over two, you're going to want to make sure you have four pairs of shoes. These should be:

- ✓ A pair of sneakers for playing and running
- ✓ A pair of rain boots in case of inclement weather
- ✓ A pair of dress shoes for more formal occasions and outings
- ✓ A pair of season-specific shoes, like sandals in the summer or non-slip boots in the winter.

CHAPTER 13:

Capsules Over 50

For the fashionista over 50, you started to realize you're growing out of your younger styles. Your body is undergoing a change, so this is a great time to re-evaluate your capsule wardrobe and build something that's comfortable for you, while still being stylish and modern.

For this, we're going to walk you through an example of a capsule wardrobe that would complement any woman over 50.

Colors

It's time to simplify. Neutral colors like black with accent tones work well in all seasons. Your wardrobe will remain stylish for years.

Stick to solids colors. If you want to add prints, stick to stripes and blocks of color.

Accessories

When shopping for accessories, focus on high-quality, versatile pieces and bigger brands for longevity and style. No costume jewelry.

Choose a handbag with a neutral silhouette as this will help define your style as it encourages your outfits to look modern and hip.

Shoes

Find shoes that are comfortable and stylish, enhancing your overall look. Your capsule wardrobe should consist of five pair shoes to transition in-between events and for daily wear.

Low wedges work well with any skirt or pant for those casual days, while mid-heels dress-up your outfit for those formal and special occasions.

Sneakers are always good to have on hand for maximum comfort; the key is not to be flashy as it'll make your outfit look childish. Aim for smart and confident.

Keeping a pair of flats in your arsenal is always wise for all ages. You can use these as a bonus accessory by wearing a bolder and patterned flat to express your individuality

With sandals, black and metallic looks are modern, especially if the straps are wide and obvious.

Bottoms

Choose pants that don't flare out too boldly and are made with a comfortable fabric. Ponte trousers, stretch jeans, and classically cut jeans won't dig into your midsection and are always current.

When looking at capris, stick to ones that crop closer to the ankle than your calf. Make sure the cut is slim or straight, a modern and purposeful look.

Dresses

Dresses are highly versatile and essential to every woman's capsule.

They can be paired with heels or strappy boots for evenings, ballet flats for an afternoon at the office, or with a solid pair of sneakers for errands and general walking.

Stick to neutrals like a black or a grey as it will give you the most options for accessorizing and layering.

Layering

Layering is more useful now than ever as it's not only used to transition the seasons, but to enhance your figure.

Blazers or short jackets are useful additions to any wardrobe and can turn most bottoms into a suit when paired. Lightweight stretch fabrics will flatter your curves.

T-shirts

Stick to softer lightweight fabrics like silk or polyester as they drape over your figure nicely without adding bulk to your shape. Try to pick t-shirts with rounder necks as they will add length to complement your neck.

As with capsules of every age, the following rules remain true:

1. Focus on **Essentials First**
2. **Quality,** Not Quantity
3. Dress for **Your Body Type**

CHAPTER 14:

Capsule Accessories

Some people shy away from accessories when they're building their capsule wardrobe because they think they contribute to the clutter we're trying to avoid. However, accessories are key components to every capsule. As we've moved along in this guide, we've included some examples of accessories. But if you want to clearly define your accessory essentials, this is the place to be.

Accessories are vital because they're the key to making our minimal wardrobe as versatile as possible while enlivening our neutral palettes.

Just as with your clothing, you want to focus on accessories that serve more than one function: they can be paired with anything and not looking out of place, and you want them to be sustainable.

For the accessory skeptic, here are reasons why you shouldn't dismiss accessories when building your capsule:

1. They're one-size-fits-all. You don't have to worry about growing out of them and they're perfect for sharing and trading with friends when you want to spice things up even further.

2. They can be reused indefinitely and paired with anything. Your long necklaces can look just as great on a dress for a dinner party and pairs with your blouse for a more laid-back

look.

3. They require little maintenance aside from an occasional polish or wipe.
4. They're small and easy to stow away, eliminating the clutter in your jewelry box.
5. They contribute to your unique style you can be proud of.

Accessory Essentials You'll Want to Have

When it comes to purses, you only need three, each one serving a unique function. For instance:

1. A clutch or wristlet for when you just need to grab your wallet and go.
2. An over-the-shoulder/satchel for casual outings.
3. An everyday handbag, like a large tote that fits all your essential items like your wallet, keys, laptop or books.

With jewelry, begin with pieces you use daily then add. Bold colors can make neutrals pop and change the look of an outfit, while silvers and golds are classic and timeless, and can work with anything.

Scarves come in a variety of fabrics and weights. A lightweight silk scarf are for warmer days, making your outfit pop or as protection from the wind, and is a great staple to have on hand. During the cooler months, a thicker wool scarf is ideal to keep warm and protection from harsh wintery winds.

Hats should be functional, first. If you live in a colder, snowy region then, you'll need to make sure you have adequate gear for the climate; whereas if you're in the south, a baseball cap will protect you from the sun.

CHAPTER 15:

Common Mistakes Shoppers Make

Building your first capsule wardrobe, although easy in concept, is often challenging. To help you avoid some of the pitfalls many people face when designing their capsule, we're going to tell you the do's and don'ts when building your capsule wardrobe and be prepared for an easy transition into your new minimalist capsule lifestyle.

The Do's of Capsule Wardrobes:

1. Plan Your Lifestyle

The prospect of starting your first capsule wardrobe is exciting and often leads many new capsule-users into a frenzy. While it's great to fantasize about the kind of clothes you'd love to wear and completely transform yourself while building your capsule, it's vital that you plan ahead for the practicality of your lifestyle. If you envision yourself as someone who wears suits and blazers to work but, in reality, work from home in casual pants and a t-shirt isn't going to help you with your capsule-building. It's important to be honest with what you will wear before committing to your capsule plan. Remember, capsules are supposed to make these kinds of decisions easier, not harder.

2. Develop Your Personal Style

Your capsule is a great opportunity to further develop your personal style. Choose pieces to reflect your current lifestyle and experiment with your style. Search on Pinterest or through your preferred magazine for additional inspiration and think about what qualities the pieces you own have that you can get in other styles that stand out to you.

3. Focus on Quality Pieces

If you don't focus on quality when you're building your capsule, all you're going to end up with is worn-out looked outfits that are falling apart at the seams. This is your chance to get sustainable, long-lasting pieces that can carry you from season to season. You'll be wearing these items more often than usual, so get ones that are built to last.

4. Organize Your Wardrobe

Regardless of how many items your capsule is made-up of, if you don't stay on top of your organization, it's going to be difficult and stressful to pick out an outfit every day. One of the main advantages of building a capsule wardrobe is how easier it is to maintain; don't slack.

The Don'ts of Capsule Wardrobes:

1. Obsess Over Numbers

One of the major reasons having a capsule wardrobe is to make the most out of a minimal amount of clothing, you'll have to consider what will work for you. A 36-piece capsule might fall just shy of your needs to be functional. It's important to recognize what will work for you and amend your capsule accordingly. It's okay to review and reassess your capsule as you go; just be mindful of the choices you're making and why.

2. Copy Someone Else's Style or Follow Trends

It's okay to use somebody else's capsule for inspiration, but copying it outright is going to do you more harm than good. When you copy someone else, or impulse buy to keep with current trends, you're not properly looking at what is functional and effective for you and your capsule. Someone who wears dresses daily is going to have a significantly different idea of a functional capsule than you might if you're always in athletic gear. Save yourself a headache and review other capsules for inspiration only, not guidelines.

3. Don't Be Too Rigid

This guide is meant to serve exactly as a guide. It is okay to find that some rules or suggested pieces outlined don't apply to you. Your wardrobe shouldn't be surrounded by rules; it should be flexible as it is organized. Want to wear a summer dress in the winter or feel like replacing your favorite t-shirt earlier than planned - go for it!

4. Don't Play It Too Safe

While building your capsule out of solid neutral colors is a great way to get yourself started, it can get dull if you play it too safe. Be sure to include a couple fun pieces to kick your wardrobe up a notch and save yourself from getting bored. Bright accessories are great for this.

Essential Shopping Tips

Inevitably, you will have to replace your pieces after they wear out. When you do, follow these three tips:

- Look for clothes that follow your current style

- Don't buy something that's the Same as your other pieces
- Make sure you love very purchase before you commit

CHAPTER 16:

The 21-Day Capsule Challenge

Now that you've taken a read through to building a capsule wardrobe, you're practically an expert who can build a capsule with their eyes closed.

The 21-day capsule challenge was designed to ease the transition into capsule wardrobes and, understandably, the premise can seem daunting to many.

If you feel ready to take on the challenge and want to dive into the fabulous world of sustainable fashion and adopt a minimalist lifestyle, it's time for the 21-day capsule challenge.

The 21-Day Capsule Wardrobe Challenge

1. Go through your wardrobe and select twenty pieces you believe will sustain you for the duration of the challenge. Since we're

just working on getting our feet wet, these items don't include your accessories, your pajamas, any workout gear or heavy outerwear, if it's cool in your region.

21-Day Challenge Example:

- 2 t-shirts (white andstripes)
- 1 ardigan (black)
- 4 blouses (white, blue, plaid, and polka dot)
- 1 blazer (red)
- 1 leather Jacket (black)
- 3 jeans (straight, skinny and bootcut denim, and black)
- 3 pants (corduroy, black, polka dot)
- 2 skirts
- 1 sress
- 1 pair of flats
- 1 pair of booties

2. Remember to try to choose pieces that are versatile and functional for your lifestyle. You will be living in them for the next 21-days after all.

3. Clean and organize your closet so that all your unused pieces are out of sight and out of mind.

4. For the next three weeks, alternate and mix and match your twenty pieces to create as many unique styles as you can. Document them, take photos, and make note of pieces that you find more versatile than others. Consider the usefulness of layering pieces, particularly if you are transitioning into a new season.

5. Use the three weeks to experiment with how far you can stretch those twenty pieces into new outfits. Play with accessories and try to avoid buying anything new. You can use this time to save money to buy capsule pieces after the three weeks.

6. In the final week of your challenge, start thinking about how you can build your next capsule. This will teach you the importance of having a working wardrobe and to look ahead in the future for transitional periods and the needs of the next season.

7. Enjoy the challenge! While you may find that twenty pieces is stressful than your current wardrobe set-up, try to have fun with it and come up with as many styles as you can. You might surprise yourself. This is only three weeks out of your life but it could save you up to a year over your lifetime!

CHAPTER 17:

The Future of Fashion

Are Capsule Wardrobes Timeless?

Capsule wardrobes are not a new phenomenon in the slightest, as before you know it we'll be celebrating its 50th year since its introduction. In that time, we have seen fashion go through drastic changes like the raising of hemlines on dresses and skirts and the lowering of waistlines, ethnic prints and psychedelic patterns on tops, and the introduction of pumps.

More recently, capsule wardrobes have seen the fashion world develop into fast-fashion, saw the degradation in the quality of materials as manufacturers quickly started to churn out new styles and marketing them to the world as necessary, despite not serving any greater function. The influx of fast fashion has made it challenging to find high-quality pieces that are as timeless as they are modern, and has significantly increased stress and anxiety in consumers everywhere.

All the while, capsule wardrobes have remained quietly in the background and adapted to global trends like shifting into more eco-conscious solutions to everyday wear.

With the advancement of social media and the dependability of the internet, capsule wardrobe began to take center stage. Socially-conscious fashion-savvy users can share their own capsules in unique and creative ways while showcasing the amazing benefits and positive impacts it had on their life. This heightened the capsule wardrobe movement and given the advantages to adopting a minimalist lifestyle in a constantly changing world. Capsule wardrobes have allowed us to take back our lives and develop a system that works for our needs, and not because there's a new trend in town.

With so much to keep up in our always on society, choosing what to wear needs take up as little time as possible so we can focus on our goals and life instead. I believe it'll always be true, and our love for capsule wardrobes will last for another fifty years.